TRICERATOPS
AND OTHER FOREST DINOSAURS

by **Dougal Dixon**

illustrated by
Steve Weston and James Field

PICTURE WINDOW BOOKS
Minneapolis, Minnesota

Picture Window Books
5115 Excelsior Boulevard
Suite 232
Minneapolis, MN 55416
877-845-8392
www.picturewindowbooks.com

Printed in the United States of America.

Library of Congress Cataloging-in-Publication Data
Dixon, Dougal.
Triceratops and other forest dinosaurs / written by
Dougal Dixon
p. cm. — (Dinosaur find)
Includes bibliographical references and index.
ISBN 1-4048-0671-7
1. Dinosaurs—Juvenile literature. 2. Forest animals—
Juvenile literature. I. Field, James, 1959- ill. II. Weston,
Steve, ill. III. Chabluk, Stefan, ill. IV. Title.
QE861.5.D67 2005
567.9—dc22   2004007309

Acknowledgments
This book was produced for Picture Window Books
by Bender Richardson White, U.K.

Illustrations by James Field (pages 4–5, 7, 13, 17, 21)
and Steve Weston (cover and pages 9, 11, 15, 19).
Diagrams by Stefan Chabluk.
All photographs copyright Digital Vision except
page 14 (Corbis Images Inc.) and page 16
(Tom Brakefield/Corbis Images Inc.).

Consultant: John Stidworthy, Scientific Fellow of the
Zoological Society, London, and former Lecturer in
the Education Department, Natural History Museum,
London.

Reading Adviser: Rosemary G. Palmer, Ph.D.,
Department of Literacy, College of Education,
Boise State University, Idaho.

Types of dinosaurs
In this book, a red shape at the
top of a left-hand page shows
the animal was a meat-eater.
A green shape shows it was
a plant-eater.

**Just how big—or small—
were they?**
Dinosaurs were many different
sizes. We have compared their
size to one of the following:

Chicken
2 feet (60 cm) tall
Weight 6 pounds (2.7 kg)

Adult person
6 feet (1.8 m) tall
Weight 170 pounds (76.5 kg)

Elephant
10 feet (3 m) tall
Weight 12,000 pounds
(5,400 kg)

TABLE OF CONTENTS

WHAT'S INSIDE?

Dinosaurs! These dinosaurs lived in forests. Find out how they survived millions of years ago and what they have in common with today's animals.

Life in the Forest

Dinosaurs lived between 230 million and 65 million years ago. The world did not look the same then. The land and seas were not in the same places. However, the forests were as deep and dark as they are today. All sorts of strange dinosaurs lived there.

A crested *Parasaurolophus*, a horned *Triceratops*, and a little *Stygimoloch* would feed on the plants in a forest. A forest had lots of hiding places. The plant-eaters had to be careful of the hungry Tyrannosaurus that watched them.

ARGENTINOSAURUS

Pronunciation:
ARE-jen-TEEN-o-SAW-rus

Argentinosaurus had a long neck to reach the treetops. It ate the tender shoots that grew there. With its comblike teeth, it raked leaves from branches.

Long necks today

Giraffes reach high trees and rake off leaves like *Argentinosaurus* did long ago.

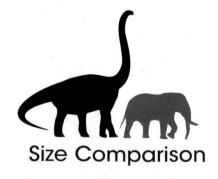

Size Comparison

No tree was too high for a group of *Argentinosaurus*. They spent their whole day eating to feed their huge bodies.

HUAYANGOSAURUS

Pronunciation:
hwi-YANG-o-SAW-rus

Huayangosaurus crashed through the forest. The plates on its back were narrow and pointed. *Huayangosaurus* could not find much to eat close to the ground. It had to look higher.

Back legs today

Male kangaroos rise on their back legs like *Huayangosaurus* did. They do so to fight.

Size Comparison

A *Huayangosaurus* stood on its hind legs to reach food. It pushed its little head into the trees.

9

MICRORAPTOR

Pronunciation:
MY-crow-RAP-tur

Microraptor had feathers on its arms and legs. It might have used its curved claws for climbing. It flew from tree to tree looking for little insects.

Feathered gliders today

A toucan often glides from tree to tree like *Microraptor* did millions of years ago.

Size Comparison

Was it a bird? Was it a bat? No, it was a *Microraptor*. It would glide through the forest.

PARASAUROLOPHUS

Pronunciation:
PAR-uh-SAW-ro-LOH-fus

Parasaurolophus used its long crest to push its way through the thick, steamy forest. It looked for juicy plants to eat. The pattern of colors on its back helped it hide from its enemies.

Pushing ahead today

Some antelope use their swept-back horns to push aside tree branches like *Parasaurolophus* once did.

Size Comparison

A *Parasaurolophus* used its crest to push branches aside. That let its big body go through the thick forest.

STYGIMOLOCH

Pronunciation:
STIG-I-MOL-uck

Stygimoloch was covered in spines and horns. They were used to frighten enemies away. *Stygimoloch* used the dome on top of its head to push others. It ate only plants.

Head-to-head today

Male warthogs look dangerous like *Stygimoloch* did. They will often head-butt their enemies.

Size Comparison

Every meat-eater was scared away by a *Stygimoloch's* looks.

15

THERIZINOSAURUS

Pronunciation:
THER-i-ZEE-nuh-SAW-rus

Therizinosaurus stood on its back legs to eat. It had claws as big as your arm. They were used to tear down branches from trees. They were also for ripping into ants' nests while looking for food.

Digging today

Anteaters use their claws to open ants' nests like *Therizinosaurus* did long ago.

Size Comparison

A *Therizinosaurus* could tear through wood or soil with its claws.

TRICERATOPS

Pronunciation:
tri-SAIR-uh-TOPS

Triceratops had a strong beak. It snipped off the tough forest plants it ate. *Triceratops* had no armor on its back. An enemy had to creep up on it from behind.

Nose pokers today

Rhinoceroses use the horns on their noses to fight off enemies like *Triceratops* once did.

Size Comparison

Nothing would attack a *Triceratops* from the front. Its head armor was too tough and its horns too sharp.

19

TYRANNOSAURUS
Pronunciation:
tie-RAN-uh-SAW-rus

Tyrannosaurus jumped out at its prey. It snapped its huge jaws and bit with its sharp teeth. Nothing escaped this dinosaur's charge. What strange little arms it had, each with only two fingers.

Big teeth today

Lions are big, fierce meat-eaters that bite with long, sharp teeth like *Tyrannosaurus* did.

Size Comparison

With a roar, hiss, or bellow, the *Tyrannosaurus* would burst from the bushes. It wanted meat for dinner.

WHERE DID THEY GO?

Dinosaurs are extinct, which means that none of them are alive today. Scientists study rocks and fossils to find clues about what happened to dinosaurs.

People have different explanations about what happened. Some people think a huge asteroid that hit Earth caused all sorts of climate changes. This then caused the dinosaurs to die. Others think volcanic eruptions caused the climate to change and that killed the dinosaurs. No one knows for sure, though.

Glossary

armor—protective covering of plates or with horns, spikes, or clubs used for fighting

beak—the hard front part of the mouth of birds and some dinosaurs

crested—with a structure on top of the head, usually used to signal to other animals

horned—with one or more pointed structures, made of bone or hair, on the head

insects—small, six-legged animals; they include ants, bees, beetles, and flies

prey—animals that are hunted by other animals for food; the hunters are known as predators

FIND OUT MORE

AT THE LIBRARY

Dixon, Dougal. *Dinosaurs: All Shapes and Sizes.* Jackson, Tenn.: Davidson Titles, 1998.

Parker, Steve. *Dinosaurs and How They Lived.* New York: Dorling Kindersley, 1992.

Pringle, Laurence. *Dinosaurs! Strange and Wonderful.* Honesdale, Pa.: Boyds Mills Press, 1995.

ON THE WEB

FactHound offers a safe, fun way to find Web sites related to this book. All of the sites on FactHound have been researched by our staff.
www.facthound.com

1. Visit the FactHound home page.

2. Enter a search word related to this book, or type in this special code: 1404806717.

3. Click on the Fetch It button.

Your trusty FactHound will fetch the best Web sites for you!

INDEX